ENGLISH AS A
SECOND LANGUAGE
AND OTHER POEMS

(*or* The Usual Entertainment)

ENGLISH AS A
SECOND LANGUAGE
AND OTHER POEMS

JASWINDER BOLINA

COPPER CANYON PRESS

PORT TOWNSEND, WASHINGTON

Cover design by Phil Kovacevich

Copper Canyon Press is in residence at Fort Worden State Park in Port Townsend, Washington, under the auspices of Centrum. Centrum is a gathering place for artists and creative thinkers from around the world, students of all ages and backgrounds, and audiences seeking extraordinary cultural enrichment.

LIBRARY OF CONGRESS CATALOGING-IN-PUBLICATION DATA
Names: Bolina, Jaswinder, 1978- author.
Title: English as a second language and other poems / Jaswinder Bolina.
Description: Port Townsend, Washington : Copper Canyon Press, [2023]
Identifiers: LCCN 2023021348 (print) | LCCN 2023021349 (ebook) |
    ISBN 9781556596575 (paperback) | ISBN 9781619322868 (epub)
Subjects: LCGFT: Poetry.
Classification: LCC PS3602.O6538 E54 2023 (print) |
    LCC PS3602.O6538 (ebook) | DDC 811/.6—dc23/eng/20230508
LC record available at https://lccn.loc.gov/2023021348
LC ebook record available at https://lccn.loc.gov/2023021349

9 8 7 6 5 4 3 2 FIRST PRINTING

COPPER CANYON PRESS
Post Office Box 271
Port Townsend, Washington 98368
www.coppercanyonpress.org

Grateful acknowledgment to the editors at the following journals where earlier versions of these poems appeared:

The Academy of American Poets Poem-a-Day: "Iguana Variations in Winter," "Probable Poem for the Furious Infant"

Allium: "The Apartment (*or* The Jesus Elegy)," "The Apology Factory"

Big Other: "Actual Elegy," "Mar-a-Lago-a-Mar," "The Old Country," "Terrible Elegy"

The Cincinnati Review: "Waiting My Turn"

Couplet Poetry: "House Hunters," "House Hunters International"

Court Green: "Bird, Elegy," "Elegy for a Dog," "A Poem, like the Soul, Which Can't Be Translated (*or* Oak Park Elegy)"

Electric Literature: "The Billy Graham Elegy"

The Fiddlehead: "A Freudian Elegy," "Once Upon a Toilet over the Alps (*or* Executive Platinum Elegy)," "Palace of Amenhotep (*or* 20th Century Elegy)"

The Gettysburg Review: "A Little Slice of Heaven," "Self-Portrait in a Baby Monitor"

The New Yorker: "Ancestral Poem"

Poetry: "English as a Second Language," "Lines Composed Upon Changing a Diaper," "The Plague on TV," "The Usual Entertainment"

Poetry Northwest: "Second City Autumnal," "A Story about the Antichrist"

Poetry London: "Desert Rose"

Porlock: "At War with the Cynics"

Sporklet: "Modern Ark"

The Volta: "Americanastan," "A Film Noir for Joseph Stiglitz"

for R.F.W.

who

among us can imagine ourselves
unimagined? who

among us can speak with so fragile
tongue and remain proud?

≈

Lucille Clifton,
"here yet be dragons"

CONTENTS

ENGLISH AS A
SECOND LANGUAGE
AND OTHER POEMS

(*or* The Usual Entertainment)

English as a Second Language

We came upon a line of English
eating dog, we thought, on plump bread
steamed and slathered with a drab yellow
chutney from a cart in the Kew Gardens.
Villains, they looked to us, offending
nature, but we asked the dog-wallah
for one apiece—me, your Gian uncle,
and the elder Sahota who held up
seven fingers, then pointed to the sky:
a code of theirs he'd broken.
The dog-wallah just shook his head,
counted our shillings, surrendered
three green glass bottles of 7UP,
three warm logs in aluminium.
In 1967, you could hear a song
by The Beatles on anybody's radio,
but what did The Beatles know about us
huddled together in our conspiracy
on a bench beneath a kind of tree
I'd never seen before? Anyway,
we were young and having fun,
the shit-eating grin on Gian's face
as we brought the dog meat to our mouths.
When you sack the villain's estate,
you have to raid the villain's kitchen.
You dress in his topcoat and drink his gin.
You set his horses free and drive them
home through the rain. You see? We weren't
afraid. We didn't come here to become
like them. We came here to eat.

It's too nice a day to read a novel set in England.

≈

David Berman,
"The Charm of 5:30"

Americanastan

At sunup, the yard rakes assembled into ranks and files
upon the common, their rusting green tines combed back,
slickened with dew. Here, they would harden a front
against the encroach of leaf blowers and riding mowers,
hickory bodies stiff in the democratic wind. Schoolkids
in uniform blues peered through windows of their ugly
yellow transports. The garages gaped open, stuffed
with croquet mallets, red metal gas canisters,
hyperrealistic Christmas statuary—a pint of Cutty Sark
embedded deep undercover in the box of lawn darts
beside the magi. A reveille of *zzzooooo*s and *zzzaaaaa*s
revved up across the hashtag architecture of suburbia.
IF YOU'RE NOT ANGRY YOU'RE NOT PAYING
ATTENTION, hollered a passing tote bag. IF YOU
WANT PEACE, WORK FOR JUSTICE, grumbled
the bumper sticker on a Cherokee. FOUR MORE YEARS,
chanted the placard leading a contrail of mentholated smoke
past the VFW. From the courthouse portico, you could see
a leaf rip its static line free of an elm tree, its jagged descent
caught in the twitchy jurisdiction of a red-light camera.

Thus began its hopeful mission to the surface;

the others would follow

Ancestral Poem

And so we settled upon the shore
of a nasally Midwestern sea
governed by a moon that hung
like a medal we'd won above
the subdivision. Evenings,
the starlings made an ecstatic
calligraphy against the gloam,
landed upon the slack, black
wires, our antique telephony
rippling between their toes.
From my vantage in a second-story
window of the split-level ranch
where we kept our things,
I could see some moths mistake
the neon heat of a Blockbuster
Video sign to the west for home,
your babaji watering the impatiens
in their beds beneath a local cosmos.
Crisscross of the pinkening contrails.
Your bibiji nursed her twilight
chai in a patio chair. She said a thing
then that made them laugh, the clouds
like painted bulls tumbling across a cave wall
in this, the only known record of these events.

House Hunters International

They'd wanted the two-story two-bath
above the creperie in De Pijp,

though they'd been willing to reconsider

the budget for old-world charm
and sleek, modern finishes in Zagreb,

a quintessential hacienda in the hills

flanking Quito, or a lanai shading
the Russian district of Phnom Penh,

but what they'd really, really wanted

was Prague in a black-and-white movie
adaptation of a book about Prague

in the '70s. They'd even read it in college.

They'd known even then they wanted
other people's architecture and pathos.

They wanted other people's transit

and squalor. They'd been prepping
for years in the burbs outside Atlanta

when a job call lit up their scopes.

They'd tracked it to this bang-on-budget
studio nestled above the ornamental

fruit stands and decorative geriatrics

occupying a piazza at the city center
of this other life they wanted to wear

like a pelt. And we watched their wanting

from a blind we'd built in our family room.
We watched as they waded, timid at first,

into the liquid crystals of the television set.

Then, more swiftly, their daggers clenched
between their teeth, they slipped beneath

its pixelated surface.

Second City Autumnal

In a dotted salwar and a pink kameez in a faux summer of late-
breaking heat in the green-carpeted kitchen, October, and her

running the pistachios and almonds into a riot in the Cuisinart
for a cache of pinni she's prepping before winter settles soon

like a chunni over the white city, but the sheer curtains billow
now warm from the windows, and her home from an overtime

shift doing data entry in Skokie, rolling out a makki ki roti to
go with the spinach, broccolini, and kale simmering into saag

in a pateela on the range, the samoseh triangulated already for
tomorrow when her sister and the family come over, and three

round baking pans of besan and barfi cooling in the oscillating
breeze of the table fan, and a siren sings in from Lincoln Square,

and the houseflies are alive for one day longer, and the boy is
asleep on a sofa under the fuzzy supervision of the television,

and she settles in finally beside him to watch *Dallas* and the ten
o'clock news, and his father will drowse home in an hour or so

from a second shift at the hydraulics factory, and they'll fuss
the boy into bed, eat late, and love each other, the fan blurring

into a blue flower, and her mumbling in her sleep, her pretty
Punjabi snoring, and her waking before the alarm bell breaks

the quiet dim she keeps for herself under the gray banner of
morning. And now who will tell her the city belongs to anyone

else? And now who will say go back where you came from?

≈

House Hunters

From a hill road above the thicket
of tanning salons, Ubers, and brewpubs

crowding the main street, she caught sight of it
at dusk in its flaxen, summer coat:

the house

like a ten-point buck nodding on a shady bank,
as if lapping from the river.

She choreographed our advance out of the west,
camouflaged in North Face jackets

and New Balance sneakers. Papa hushed
the baby strapped to his chest in a BabyBjörn.

At a quarter klick, he signaled for us
to egress the realtor's Escalade.

The elder children knew to hide
our numbers in a single file.

She winked to us once
before cocking her musket,

our doting mother,
crack shot and immigrant on the hunt.

A Poem, like the Soul, Which Can't Be Translated (*or* Oak Park Elegy)

Optimism's a funny color on a couple of Virgos,
but here we go retiling the powder room in quartz
again as if industry is rewarded by anything
other than industry in the middle of all this
whatever-this-is. First aperitifs, then crudités.
First boxed wine, then chitchat, over cakes,
of an almost imperceptible candor. Thus
the seasons bustle onward rebranding themselves
so the Weber and Kingsford people keep extending
their ad buys deeper into pumpkin-picking
pigskin weather, and we feel weirdly sweaty
disemboweling a turkey on an island
in the kitchen when the older kid says,
*Momma, I'monna need a doper raincoat in this pisspot
of a winter.* It gets so you wish there were actual
barbarians at the gate, anyone to crush with a mace,
but there is no gate, not one guy in a pelt
banging with any malice; just dad bods
and threenagers storming the bouncy castle.
And a magician at the party keeps disappearing
the rabbits and doves, but we can see plain as day
how he does it, snapping their necks,
tossing them over his shoulder—simple as that!
Don't blame me, cupcake, I voted for the other guy.
But somebody still has to pay for this shit.

The Apology Factory

I've been fabricating my sweet apology
for package and delivery, riveting the fins
to its fuselage, hand-stitching its checkered
little nose cone, soldering the intimate circuits
into its motherboard on the graveyard shift
between Kellyanne who mans the Begging
Your Pardon machine and White Mike
on the I Meant No Offense press,
and the PA system is fucked repeating,
We'd like to thank you for your attention . . .
so we start humming along as if it's a song
we all know by heart. One factory over,
they forge-weld self-righteous suicide pacts.
Next door to that, they distill drunken marriage
proposals. But here, we work on our failings.
We get to the bottoms of our problems.
You can note the telltale slump
in our postures. You can detect the hint
of a quaver picked up by my lapel mic
as I hammer out your bent feelings,
assemble my regrets into a functional scale
model of how sorry I am for misunderstanding
how sensitive you are, how sensitive the subject,
and how offended you seem, how sorry I am
that you seem to take everything so personally,
but it's like we always say around this place,
if you aren't in some kind of trouble,
you're probably part of the problem, which,
I can assure you, we're redoubling
our best efforts to correct.

A Freudian Elegy

"The opposite of God is a question God isn't the answer to,"

the boy tells his goldfish as he X-Actos
inkblots out of his psychiatry

                                        textbook. Each is a picture
                            of his mother at various phase shifts

in her waveform, and he aims
to hang them down the wall

                                        along the stair. Here she is licking
                                        white frosting from a spatula

and here shrieking at his bedside
                            and here Frenching someone obscure

in her girlhood duplex in Baltimore.
                                        Here is some tubing garlanded

to an IV pole she grips like a trusty
harpoon at her side. *I will spike the whale,*

                                        she glares into the camera.
Her hospital socks make sad

                                        galoshes, so by the time he wades
down into the kitchen, he's sick

                                        almost to death, thinking of her,
                                        but here she is, years removed

from any of that, now buttery,
now bright as a biscuit,

                                        killing her Parliament
                              in a ramekin before toweling off

her throwing hand on her Johnny
Unitas jersey and embracing him

                              as if he is moving to Indianapolis.
When she catches sight of herself

                                        in his facsimile of her
eyes, she gasps and asks—

            O God, what was it she asked?

A Story about the Antichrist

"The opposite of transubstantiation is a yeast infection
       just as the opposite of wine is the grape seed
born of a grape fuck," the Antichrist had offered
       to her SAT prep instructor, which is how
she'd landed in detention now wondering
       whether a bordeaux or a zin converted more
readily into platelet and plasma. It must vary
       by vintner and vessel, she thought, carving
a tiny upside-down cross into her desk
       with a raw corner of her switchblade comb.
She'd been itching for a Coors and a long draw
       off the joint in her sock, and she prayed to Christ
the dean hadn't ratted her out to the homefolk,
       as if Christ were more than just an idea, but she knew
Christ was just an idea, and she still thought it was weird
       she'd never read a single elegy for the guy
except in the way the whole religion is an elegy
       for the guy, which she mostly admired
for its choral arrangements and galloping pastors,
       for how it kept mistaking epileptics for saints
or for demons, for its unrepentant gore and the soft
       lighting of the midnight mass at Christmas
and the blood in its cups and the flesh on its tongues,
       none of which she would change a bit,
she thought. She'd do it all exactly the same.

Mar-a-Lago-a-Mar

If we aren't guilty of ignorance, we're guilty of evil,

we giggle to each other at the hotel bar
the color of a sea the color of wisteria pretty

as the past where we will live one day

upon a flotilla of detergent bottles upon
that sea, breezy as the dilettantes of history

which is rich with wisteria and dilettantes

drinking Sazeracs in hotel bars that used to be
so well regarded when white people wore their finest

laundry and ate snails there, chortling *regatta*

or *eugenic* or *frittata* at one another,
and now all of that is lost to the progress

that is as unnerving and relentless

as it is relentless and unnerving,
its infants arriving insolvent,

demanding succor, new weirdos

ascendant, the progress insistent as a refugee
or a tidewater or the whole of the thunderful sea rising

to eat us, we giggle, like we wouldn't eat it first!

Once Upon a Toilet over the Alps (*or* Executive Platinum Elegy)

I'd rather die of a heart attack in the can at thirty-nine
thousand feet, I said to the receptionist at my kid's ear,
nose, and throat guy, than by drowning in the head
of a Benetti on the Med. But I'm soused with incredulity

now having that heart attack in the can of a Dreamliner
to Milan via Copenhagen, and Alan Cumming is on
this flight! I have so many questions for Alan,
who features so prominently in two of my four

favorite films I'd been watching all in a row
on demand over a brioche roll and Thai noodle salad.
O heart, don't shuck me now I've been upgraded
and for nothing but my mileage bonus, which I earned—

I and not all these organs capitulating to some other,
indecipherable obligation, and in business class no less
where I've long sought to pamper all my viscera;
I don't deserve their revolting! my brain keeps shrieking

inside of itself at six hundred miles per hour, once upon a toilet
over the Alps, those Swiss and indifferent mountains
I won't mogul again, Alan, help, Alan, help—

Modern Ark

He he he he and he and he and and he and he and he and and
as and as he and as he and he.

Gertrude Stein, "If I Told Him:
A Completed Portrait of Picasso"

My dachshund Manet and her sister
Monet and my sweet chinchilla Kandinsky
and the gerbil Cézanne and my gecko
Gauguin and my budgie Marcel Duchamp

with my ferret Matisse, my tarantula Ernst,
the guinea pigs Pollock and Rothko, and Banksy
the dove, Andy Warhol the newt, with my parakeets
Haring and Twombly, and my box turtle Jasper,

my calico Vince, my Shetland Willem de Kooning,
and my betta fish Jean flicks his fins in the back
of the Mack with my bed and my couch,
my dumbbells, my absinthe, and laudanum

in our big hairy rig on the A68, the hills throbbing green
as a sea between manly Toulouse and tiny, medieval Lautrec.

Elegy for a Dog

Your use of *synergy* in the absence of any irony
contributed more than a little to the divorce,

and your insistence on *to be frank, the sixties, as it were,*

and other such phrases you'd tic out while the rest of us
shuddered, how you'd lean in real breathy

to say, *Gimme the straight dope, sweetheart,*

to the cashier in the A&W like you were a couple
of rocket stages nestled into each other,

and that you boned other people didn't help,

but we couldn't, just couldn't stomach any longer
your reveries on Joyce and on Mailer, on scotch

and Larry Bird, your insistence on analog audio

equipment on which you'd mostly play bootlegs
of Bob Dylan, oozingly, insistently calling him

DYlin like he was a beloved Labrador struck

by a Coke truck, and you in your beat-up Chucks,
your cowlick, and Levi's, bearing the dog corpse

out of a ditch to bury beneath the ole willow tree.

You tell everyone that story, how you're still that kid
the old man called *squirt* those fatted hours

when bread cost a nickel and a paper cost a nickel

and a Buick cost a dime, and all Minnesota reeked
like an overstuffed ashtray, but in a good way,

you'd say, your corned teeth flashing, the vein

in your temple coursing like a tiny Mississippi
out of the wispy white laurel of your last hairdo,

which are all things we could've overlooked

for a little less cliché in your Converse, a little more
rigor in your ditties, *But that's just the way things were*

back in those days, you'd say back in those days things were

exactly the way you said they were.

Waiting My Turn

Honestly, Elizabeth, I think I'd rather be the 239th
Jaswinder on the moon than the 1st,

rather myself an *n*th brown anybody
in a hand-me-down helmet, a secondhand

pressure suit, my capsule certified
and pre-owned, the dull interns yawning

at their stations in the humdrum easy
of ground control, my khaki booster

routinely returning to rest on its pad,
otherworldly for its exertion for sure,

but when it says, "Boy, I seen *everything,*
boys," to the gleaming white rockets,

they're gassing up, readying for Neptune,
snickering, "The *moon*?? Everybody's been

to the goddamn moon," though I am 239,000
miles out of earshot, stepping onto the lethal grit

of the goddamned *moon,* beaming, "At last.

It's *my* fucking turn at last."

The Living Daylights (*or* A Passage to Indiana)

"I'll beat the living daylights out of you,"
she says, his blond head banged up

against the blackboard, his collar squirting
blue between her brown knuckles,

but later that summer, their pinkies graze
in the chlorinated heat of the park district

pool. Their hands clasp sweaty beneath
a picnic table outside the Super Dawg.

Endorphin, milkshake, endorphin,
cheese fry, she feels the first warm

sphincter-tingle of love. O hormonal
light, the nights chirp through her nightly

until the morning of the Fourth when
he randomly dumps her for Nicole

Something-Or-Other in the gazebo
behind the war memorial. *Fuck,* mutters

the gut through its nauseous hollows.
Puke, burble the heart's gory hydraulics.

Nothing will ever be good again, she thinks.
But she chuckles thinking on it now,

so many election cycles later, at the umber end
of summer, thinking on him and Nicole

maybe together still in a bungalow somewhere,
Fort Wayne maybe, teeming with plump

little Something-Or-Others, toaster waffles
and coffee, their table gummy with syrup,

their youngest burbling something maybe,
their youngest named maybe sentimentally

for her: plump little Sukhdeep Kaur
Something-Or-Other in her high chair.

And I'll bet you something, she thinks.
I'll bet she's their favorite.

A Film Noir for Joseph Stiglitz

She'd wearied of the gruff interrogations
and pithy rejoinders, had answered twice

every dick combing the manor,

so she sat twiddling a last hexahedron of ice
watering the gin in her *Life's a Beach!* coffee mug.

Down cellar, a mild-mannered roach
checked into a homicidal motel.

Everyone she'd ever known had settled

in for an evening of Netflix and edibles,

and earthquakes were more common
than sex in the dry county that year,

which is why she took hold of the lieutenant's nape
like a candlestick telephone,

pulled his hard-boiled ear in close,
and murmured, *Because who would miss*

a dead supply-side macroeconomist lying

like a shadow on a rug
in the leather and varnished interior of his Victorian study?

Terrible Elegy

Compassion is no substitute for justice.

> Rush Limbaugh (d. 17 February 2021),
> 18 February 1994

I believe a person can celebrate the death of a terrible person
and not be a terrible person,

that it'd take a princely vintage of arrogance to worry
one's marginal guts might get rung up by a hypercritical

lightning and for so minor and sentimental an infraction
upon a landscape so littered with heavy, metal

monuments to Stonewall Jackson and Andrew Jackson,
beneath the president like a heavy metal broadcast

antenna above the law in its metal-heavy riot gear.
And it might take a dafter brand of arrogance to believe

one would not be struck down like a thick man
looming alone with an 8-iron on an ominous fairway,

but I have neither motive nor opportunity
to determine which of these applies in your terrible case,

so raucous and high am I in the conga line
at the luau on the night of your fantastic passing

not even the least terrible among us should lament,
cha-cha-cha.

Lately, I've become accustomed to the way
The ground opens up and envelops me
Each time I go out to walk the dog.
Or the broad edged silly music the wind
Makes when I run for a bus . . .

Things have come to that.

≈

Amiri Baraka,
"Preface to a Twenty Volume
Suicide Note"

The Billy Graham Elegy

Nobody much mentions the floor of the Sistine Chapel
that's touched so many more than the docents or the ceiling
or the premonitions on the wall. Come papal loafer
and heathen sneaker, come Ked and ECCO mingling dog
shit off the viale e strada on this scuffed stone nobody
mentions much as the tourist kids keep calling it
"The Sixteen Chapel" as if it were one more middling outlet
in a protracted franchise, which it is, which must be why
the Lord doesn't appear here much more than elsewhere,
retired as he must be to Ostia as is custom among Romans.
One can't, after all, be messiah forever. Eventually,
the ball club needs a fresh message, a fresher messenger,
fella in a silk suit maybe, a Carolina drawl, maybe
another mother appointed chairwoman of the Pietà.
But we don't think much of home among the Alfa
Romeos of the military police here where we're unafraid
anyone will shoot us, and Rome feels comprehensible
for once. I know how to say, "Vorrei due cornetti,"
or, "Mia moglie è incinta," or, "Dov'è il bancomat?"
abbiamo soldi for once in our lives, and the taxi
drivers of evening tell me, "Your Italian is so good,
where do you come from?" But the taxi drivers
of morning say, "Your Italian is so bad, di dove sei?"
I don't tell either we're from the outcome, a new world
and latter result, that all this artistry ends in half a nation
mourning a holy mogul in a circus tent, and mercifully
nobody there comes back from the dead.

All His Fascist Wants

"It's as if we want to believe the fascist
is entirely the man on TV

when the fascist is mostly the man watching

the man on TV wanting what the fascist wants,"
I'd been telling the boy

when he broke squealing free

of the containment zone we'd attempted
around the tub, and hurtled through

the naked chambers of our modest regime,

and we were hopeless then to stop him,
we said to each other, so mad were we

with affection at his indomitable overthrow,

his adorable unrelenting. After all, we said,
we'd invited him into this rapt world,

and the world is all he wanted.

Self-Portrait in a Baby Monitor

A gleaming through the blinds organizes the ceiling into a spreadsheet of light above you whimpering in your plush cell with the Steiff monkey we call Bowie mugging for the camera on the wall, and me drowsing on a knee beside the crib, one animal petting another animal, singing you miserably to sleep,   and I'm bored, so I listen for the Metro rumble through the window.   I make believe a tundra in the rug, an artisan stitching the last uptick of a smile into Bowie's face before he padlocks his workshop and plods through snowdrifts home to hang his lederhosen on a peg beside the hearth.   His children are asleep in a bunk room down the hall, a German shepherd dozing on a bearskin rug, as he ladles himself some stew from a pot in his ember-lit great room then settles into the settee to oil their mother's bunions to Ziggy Stardust crooning over the gramophone.   "Life is made like this," she says, checking the baby monitor before resting her head on an armrest, "of the crackling proximity of bodies to other bodies," and he agrees it must be true as it's true between them now.   But to accept any of this, you'd have to believe the monkeys aren't assembled by a thousand women in Sidi Bouzid, then shipped to Giengen for their Warenzeichen and exported via container ship across a blank sea   where it is night now,   a steward stepping out of the mess to light his Gaulwaz, his fingers cupping the flame to his face so the salt of the middle Atlantic mingles with the smoke in his nose to spark a memory of his mother home from the factory floor peering in on his sleep with an oil lamp.   Scattershot of the cosmos. A satellite rolls over.   He imagines she's there watching him now in the grayscale of her monitor at central command, reporting on his progress to her superiors.   I wonder if they're impressed. I'd like to tell them that his mission succeeded, that Bowie made it, that he's here beside you now in your bad sleep, looking up at me kneeling in the third person of a night-vision screen, his countenance fixed grinning into the middle distance, his dumb, animal joy unrelenting.

A Little Slice of Heaven

"Because it'd only make sense for the thing you feel least
       in the afterlife to be the thing you felt most

in the current life, though you have to admit if there's
       an afterlife, it'd probably mean this life is a reckoning

for some prior execution, which means this shitshow might
       be exactly the penance we deserve," she said,

which seemed, even to me, an odd stab at small talk,
       even for a madcap pediatrician,

but, Alakazam! she pronounced the baby perfectly

healthy and ordered him another round of shots
       before deploying us to another six-month stint

in the wild, but that thing she said really stuck with me sitting
       there beside you the whole bus ride home and later

feeding the baby a bowlful of consolidated peas and carrots
       and beside you in bed until morning,

and the days peeled away like that, like platitudes from
       a quote-a-day calendar, like rounds of a deli loaf

off a slicer in the deli, like cross sections of the cortex cut
       clean by an MRI, and it really stuck in my head,

that thing she said, and it probably always will until
       I acquit myself of the grist of this life and submit

myself to the next one where I may never feel again as I do
       beside you tonight sopping up bouillabaisse,

my serious love, with the soft guts
       of a baguette on a Friday night in this life

I must've qualified for and justly received,
       I know not the hokey jurisprudence of why.

Desert Rose

after H.D.

Sentimental the skink
makes a lifetime
with one and not another.
So the desert is mine—

moon in heat, gilded
browning—everything
crackles, everything
hushes up, blues the dunes,

tepid night,
the dung beetle
navigating by galaxy
steers its tiny, round turd
along a sextant of stars

as if this were the nuclear point
of their fusion, which it is—
how I love you.

Bird, Elegy

after Constantin Brâncuși

Today we found a bird,

you and I, splayed
like a ragged umbrella,

in our bathrobes

on the balcony after
a hootenanny of a storm,

is something I can't say

in painting or in sculpture,
in French or Romanian,

it being impossible to translate
my cheesy, midwestern

grief into mixed media,

and I don't know French
or Romanian, I must confess

in English to you and the baby

perched in his Jumperoo™,
while I am plucking

the bird's body clean

off our rancid stucco
with a grocery bag,

and I think he understands me,

the baby, though he doesn't speak
Romanian or French or English;

he only knows painting

and sculpture, not the words,
but the contours of sorrow,

poor little guy, alighted

into what he doesn't know
is America, a Saturday

in May on a planet—

he doesn't know
what a fucking planet is!

—the silver blimp drifting

above us like a grayscale
sketch of a bird in flight,

like a conceptual rubber ducky,

which is the opposite
of this stiff hanky

crumpled like a gray equation

upon the patio
upon which I adore you

because you can't stop sobbing,

your tears are shiny bronze
figurines in the gallery

of your face, imploring,
What chance does any of us have?

But the baby disagrees

and meeps, *Bonne chance,*
mes petits oiseaux,

bonne chance!

Hidden Valley Ranch

The night mare trotted into a clearing
where I'd fallen asleep,

her clackety wagon filled with snakes
and shame and everything precious to me.

I should've done something,
but I kept snoozing like a drunk Sunday

with three stories of an apartment building
suspended above me and you and the baby

in his potato sack in the bassinet.
I didn't do a thing as the night

mare nuzzled him, her whinny glinting
some kind of moonlight,

as she snorted and whined until
he leapt up! took hold of her mane,

and they galloped off together
through a gap in the teeth of the curtains

as I gasped and gasped from the bed
I rode like a Conestoga unhitched

and careering deep into the outlaw night.

The Bad News: A Film Noir

Now traipsing down a boulevard, now vaulting

over a turnstile, now clicking its heels
up the steps to the Elevated, then down

the line to my postal code, now arriving

in my dingy lobby in its gator-skin
jacket and velveteen loafers,

the Bad News hot-wires the buzzer,

invites itself up with its bouquet of wild
aneurysms and drooping embolisms,

florid accidents and petite melanomas,

and it isn't welcome here,
but the Big Bad News screeches

its bad emergency alert into my regularly

scheduled broadcast. Now
my every chyron reads: YOU'RE FUCKED!

beneath a bad anchor with a bad hairdo

reporting how badly fucked I am
by the Fucked-Up Furious News breaking

down my door, its tommy gun trained

on my head in my human apartment
stocked with toiletries and rations,

its earnest furniture and photographs

of my son and our mothers
who machined us inside themselves,

our mothers who delivered us,

like armored personnel carriers,
to our stations in the world,

but the Abominable News will dismantle them all

soon as it's finished with me
with my back to the door,

my hi-fi cranking its earthly music,

gorgeous me running the blender
on a daquiri: *buzzzzz, buzzz, buzz.*

The Plague on TV

The kid keeps asking if there are rhetorical questions
in the afterlife, and does the little voice go on chattering
inside the headless? In whose language? Do the gods pray
to one another? What do they ask for? What do they offer
to sacrifice? It's the 29th of February, a cicada droning
on the sill and a plague on TV and the kid going on and on,
but it feels good to sit here buzzing inside myself watching
TV at the odd end of Florida, February, a cicada moaning
on the sill and a plague on and the kid going on and on,
so I go on debating with myself whether it'd be better
to die of the plague or to die of anything other than
the plague during a plague, and I begin getting nervous
for the kid and for myself as remembered by the kid
riding shotgun in the lead car behind my hearse,
and I begin to wonder how long I'll miss the view
from inside my own head in any kind of afterlife,
of the other side of my face, of the kid as seen
through my face, of TV and the cicada like a little
winged ambulance bawling on the sill purpling
with dusk, meaning my view of everything, I keep
asking and asking, but the kid's decamped to his bunk,
the cicada receded into the soft quarantine of night,
and the TV is talking to itself again, and the plague is there
making its gross calculations like a god sizing up a lamb.

Quarantine Bardo

for R.A.

Then today, we debated the selective logics
of cannibalism over hot dogs on the fire escape.

Ragtag squadrons of houseflies
gathered at the screen door plotting
a next daring incursion. Like a suicide cult
with attention deficit disorder, we quipped.

Pesky nucleotides dropped anchor all along
the coasts of our bodies, but people were still
out walking their dogs and kids.

A neighbor we once knew set up
her celesta on the stoop and played
John Prine covers all evening long,

so all evening long, a live music stole
across the terrain, off the urgent care
clinic and through the bank drive-thru
before it infiltrated the ironwork fencing
the cemetery beneath the El tracks.

A train flew over.

Nobody was on it but me.

≈

The Apartment (*or* The Jesus Elegy)

This is when it occurs to him Jesus must've had an apartment

too—zydeco and bacon steam gusting between the buildings,
the morning anchor announcing summer's hot emergencies

from a snowy Zenith in the other room. Unless, he guesses,

He'd surfed the disciples' futons or freeloaded off His Parents
deep into His reluctant Manhood. But probably not. Probably

Jesus hustled all through His strapped twenties, shuffled home late

to a stark efficiency walking distance from bars, markets,
and baths, the militant fisheries and insurgent cafés, nothing but

a sleeping mat upon His floor. Nothing but a pillow that never

tasted a woman. Not a lick of tequila in the entire Mother-
loving place. He'd come alone from His shifts running barback

at the brothel to wash His feet, to slurp His dahl and stare

into the sliver of astronomy in His little lancet window, not
smoking, not listening to Sam Cooke, not touching Himself

as He plotted His Own Execution. Sundays, Peter would bang

on the door to rouse Him early, to dish on the gang or tempt
Him into a walk by the sea. They'd fry up a few sardines first

to eat on pita without speaking. Peter would've missed that

the most, he thinks, after He'd gone: the quiet alone together,
quiet and alone save the mewing of a cat in the alley between

tenement shacks, not a body but Jesus mewing back.

Actual Elegy

I'm trying to say something that feels like hearing
your voice for the first time.

It isn't working. I keep ending up at myself,

the part of myself that accidentally believes
in g-d sometimes, like how I killed a June bug

that yesterday abruptly landed on my neck

then sat up half the night in a chair
asking the ceiling fan to forgive me

as if all it propellered aloft might drop down
and crush my every sin then and there.

It didn't. I'm still here.
And you never are.

Which is the trouble with this place

The Old Country

The APR on the Sapphire Visa is bringing me down

and the mania of the evening commute
is bringing me down and the talk radios

of the yokel electorate are bringing me down,

so I'm a bogged log in a rainforest of traffic
bringing me down between the semis

and Civics in the local lanes of the tollway

upon which it rains tonight
like it rains everywhere every night

except in the Atacama Desert where it hardly rains at all,

rock salts glitter in a high wind, and we shiver,

my donkey and me, arriving at a puddle
round and shallow as a rocks glass,

and kneeling beside him, I give

his oafish ear a tug toward the drink
which he refuses in favor of me

who loved him most of all that I deserted

in that desert home we called home,
lo, those many deserts ago.

Palace of Amenhotep (*or* 20th Century Elegy)

No pharaoh does miss his kitty any more
than I miss the dive bars of Chicago, 1998,
wood-paneled, red-lettered, dank and cozy
as confessional booths, with a single, knobbed
television in one corner and an elder
in a respirator ad on mute between innings
when I couldn't, I couldn't, I couldn't imagine
my face affixed to a breathing machine,
I'd say to the cigarette machine, yanking
hard, and out bounded a pack of Camels,
but I could've, I could've, I could've
imagined it if bleating youth could've
permitted more than obsessing over other
people's underpants, prime-time dramaturgy,
shooting Old Crow until 4 a.m. home
to the cat I called Amenhotep, and not
in honor of the guy. Good old Amenhotep
would've gnawed my nose clean off
if she'd caught me on a savanna
instead of our great apartment enflanneled
as it was then by loneliness for a whole year
that lasted seven years, so I really felt much older
by the end of it but not any wiser, Amenhotep
ever indifferent to my every want and affection,
and affection is what I wanted most
to give as the century ended like a dynasty
into a perfect ruin where I am, to this day,
gutted, wrapped, and doggedly intact
as a cat in a cat-shaped coffin.

Iguana Variations in Winter

They may fall from the trees, but they are not dead.

National Weather Service Miami

don't mistake for suffering what isn't suffering | the hint of
a chill tossing some palms

—

me in a frumpy green sweater | the iguanas swooning
in verdant afghans

—

limp and leather | a flurry of iguanas startled the road

—

atop an emerald Lexus plopped the iguana ! the snowbirds
mistook it for a chameleon driving through their lush resort

—

like a sculpture of itself | the iguana depicted stillness

without any fear of stillness

—

I'm afraid of many things | but none is the iguana
lying naked on a swale in its dead dream of winter

At War with the Cynics

O night! I'm too sad to sing
my petulant arias, I can't stand

the sound of my own blubbering!
O night, make me something

other than I am now, mopey
though the chipper crickets

play leggy violins inside you,
the owls are stout concertinas

puffed up hooting, your zephyrs
xylophoning gator spines

in the glades before rushing up
to tease me in my bleak office

like bawdy ditties from faraway
festivals I'm not privy to!

O night, I'm tired of talking
about myself, tell me more

about you with your blue
Neptunes and red Betelgeuses,

your eternities with too little
inside them! O night, must I be

lonely and mad forever? At least
we have each other, O night,

like the baby has his blankie
coiled all around him,

but even the baby is tangled
up in my sorrow, O night,

I have too much to love
and not long enough to love it!

O night, make me something
other than all my incessant

glooming in the dappled Florida
dark where the parrots roost dopey

in the bosoms of gumbo-limbo
trees until squawking morning when

they brunch on maggots and seeds,
bomb lilied shits upon our sedans,

then soar off to Bimini!

Lines Composed Upon Changing a Diaper

Marian upstairs is anxious for an update

from the extended care facility
where her husband is dying.

Four blue macaws bustle through
the airspace above the neighborhood.

Her footfalls go cursing from room to room.

Here, the toddler testifies,
"*Noooo* poops!"

But the toddler is lying.

I tell him there are nine spiders living inside
the walls for every person in a building.

They spin their twilit colonies

in an alternate dimension rippling
beneath the drywall.

Termites romancing in the joists.

We worry about so much
more than ourselves, I tell him.

But, I tell him, it'll all be alright,
because it'll all be alright,

though not all of us will live long enough to agree.

One night, we hear Marian's husband has broken
back into himself through a skylight in his own mind

demanding to see his wife again, demanding
the nurses release him again,

demanding a Reuben from a diner
in Brooklyn that folded in 1996,

but by morning, he's ghosted
back into his framework.

From the exterior view, your birth is
exactly as inevitable as your death.

I know not the schematics of why, baby,
but I remain devoted to my task,

wiping you clean, buttoning you up,
answering your every complaint

with a grammar you don't understand.

Probable Poem for the Furious Infant

I put on the June leaves of the boulevards
I stepped out of my thoughts of death

Nâzim Hikmet,
"I Stepped Out of My Thoughts
of Death"

Probably you'll solve gravity, flesh out our microbiomics,
        split our God

particles into their constituent bits of christs and antichrists
        probably,

probably you'll find life as we know it knitted into every nook
        of the prattling

cosmos, quaint and bountiful as kismet and gunfights in the
        movies probably,

probably, probably you have no patience for the movies there
        in your eventual

arrondissement where you have more credible holography,
        more inspiring

actual events, your ghazals composed of crow racket,
        retro-rockets, your glaciers

breaking, your discotheques wailing probably, probably,
       probably, probably

too late a sentient taxi airlifts you home over the refurbished
       riverbank

beside the rebuilt cathedral, your head dozing easy in the
       crook of your arm,

emptied of any memory of these weeks we haven't slept,
       you've been erupting

into that hereafter like a hydrant on fire, like your mother is
       an air raid, and I am

an air raid, and you're a born siren chasing us out of your
       airspace, we've caught

forty-seven daybreaks in thirty-seven days probably, and you,
       little emissary, arrived

to instruct us, we wake now you shriek us awake, we sleep
       now you give us to sleep.

Little lost and gentle soul,
companion and guest of the body,
get ready now to go down into
colourless, arduous and bare places
where you will no longer have the usual entertainment.

≈

Publius Aelius Hadrianus, 138

English translation of
French translation of Latin
attributed to Marguerite
Yourcenar, *Memoirs of
Hadrian,* 1951, as transcribed
from a placard at Castel
Sant'Angelo, Rome, 2018,
translator unknown

The Usual Entertainment

How the sweat-drenched vendors hawk
Old Styles to the drunken disorderlies—

who are us!—in the pilsner light
of August buzzing with gnats and lingo,

the umpire barking his commandments
like a clergyman, the manager barking back

like a heretic. I douse my dog in ketchup
and buy me some peanuts and Cracker Jack

just for the toy and a small blue helmet
of soft serve for Jorge and a Polish for Mike

and three cold-slicked beers numbing our thumbs
in the upper mezzanines of the food chain

in the city of my heart, Illinois, where we lose
so much more than we win, but whatever the score,

I say, what good is the soul without its tongue
and its teeth, without its nose for the cut of the grass,

its ear for the hum on the air, without its words
and no throat to holler them out of to everyone

glittering here in the sticky of the cheap seats?

THE USUAL ENTERTAINMENT

(or English as a Second Language and Other Poems)

CONTENTS

≈

≈

What book will you be reading when you die?
If it's a good one, you won't finish it.
If it's a bad one, what a shame.

≈

Mary Ruefle,
"Merengue"

for T.W.B.

ABOUT THE AUTHOR

Jaswinder Bolina is author of the poetry collections *The 44th of July,*
Phantom Camera, and *Carrier Wave,* of the digital chapbook *The Tallest*
Building in America, and of the essay collection *Of Color.* His essays can
be found at *The Washington Post, The Paris Review,* the Poetry Foundation,
and other outlets. His poems have appeared in *Poetry, The New Yorker,*
Ploughshares, and elsewhere.

Lannan Literary Selections

For two decades Lannan Foundation has supported the publication and distribution of exceptional literary works. Copper Canyon Press gratefully acknowledges their support.

LANNAN LITERARY SELECTIONS 2023

Jaswinder Bolina, *English as a Second Language and Other Poems*

Natalie Eilbert, *Overland*

Amanda Gunn, *Things I Didn't Do with This Body*

Paisley Rekdal, *West: A Translation*

Michael Wiegers (ed.), *A House Called Tomorrow: Fifty Years of Poetry from Copper Canyon Press*

RECENT LANNAN LITERARY SELECTIONS FROM
COPPER CANYON PRESS

Chris Abani, *Smoking the Bible*

Mark Bibbins, *13th Balloon*

Jericho Brown, *The Tradition*

Victoria Chang, *Obit*

Victoria Chang, *The Trees Witness Everything*

Leila Chatti, *Deluge*

Shangyang Fang, *Burying the Mountain*

Nicholas Goodly, *Black Swim*

June Jordan, *The Essential June Jordan*

Laura Kasischke, *Lightning Falls in Love*

Deborah Landau, *Soft Targets*

Dana Levin, *Now Do You Know Where You Are*

Philip Metres, *Shrapnel Maps*

Paisley Rekdal, *Nightingale*

Natalie Scenters-Zapico, *Lima :: Limón*

Natalie Shapero, *Popular Longing*

Arthur Sze, *The Glass Constellation: New and Collected Poems*

Fernando Valverde, *America* (translated by Carolyn Forché)

Michael Wasson, *Swallowed Light*

Matthew Zapruder, *Father's Day*

Poetry is vital to language and living. Since 1972, Copper Canyon Press has published extraordinary poetry from around the world to engage the imaginations and intellects of readers, writers, booksellers, librarians, teachers, students, and donors.

WE ARE GRATEFUL FOR THE MAJOR SUPPORT PROVIDED BY:

academy of american poets

THE PAUL G. ALLEN
FAMILY FOUNDATION

 amazon *literary partnership*

 POETRY FOUNDATION

4 CULTURE

Lannan

 the point envision·enact·evolve

 ART WORKS. National Endowment for the Arts arts.gov

WASHINGTON STATE
ARTS COMMISSION

 A& OFFICE OF ARTS & CULTURE
SEATTLE

  The Witter Bynner Foundation
for Poetry

TO LEARN MORE ABOUT UNDERWRITING
COPPER CANYON PRESS TITLES,
PLEASE CALL 360-385-4925 EXT. 103

WE ARE GRATEFUL FOR THE MAJOR SUPPORT PROVIDED BY:

Richard Andrews and
  Colleen Chartier
Anonymous
Jill Baker and Jeffrey Bishop
Anne and Geoffrey Barker
Donna Bellew
Will Blythe
John Branch
Diana Broze
John R. Cahill
Sarah Cavanaugh
Keith Cowan and Linda Walsh
Stephanie Ellis-Smith and
  Douglas Smith
Mimi Gardner Gates
Gull Industries Inc.
  on behalf of William True
William R. Hearst III
Carolyn and Robert Hedin
David and Jane Hibbard
Bruce S. Kahn
Phil Kovacevich and Eric Wechsler

Lakeside Industries Inc.
  on behalf of Jeanne Marie Lee
Maureen Lee and Mark Busto
Ellie Mathews and Carl Youngmann
  as The North Press
Larry Mawby and Lois Bahle
Hank and Liesel Meijer
Petunia Charitable Fund and
  adviser Elizabeth Hebert
Madelyn S. Pitts
Suzanne Rapp and Mark Hamilton
Adam and Lynn Rauch
Emily and Dan Raymond
Joseph C. Roberts
Cynthia Sears
Kim and Jeff Seely
D.D. Wigley
Barbara and Charles Wright
In honor of C.D. Wright,
  from Forrest Gander
Caleb Young as C. Young Creative
The dedicated interns and faithful
  volunteers of Copper Canyon Press

The pressmark for Copper Canyon Press
suggests entrance, connection, and interaction
while holding at its center
an attentive, dynamic space for poetry.

This book is set in Arno Pro.
Book design by Phil Kovacevich.
Printed on archival-quality paper.

THE USUAL ENTERTAINMENT

JASWINDER BOLINA

COPPER CANYON PRESS
PORT TOWNSEND, WASHINGTON

THE USUAL ENTERTAINMENT

(*or* English as a Second Language and Other Poems)